Salimata Traore Rawlings

Phoenix: Metamorphosis

Salimata Traore Rawlings

Phoenix: Metamorphosis

Poetry

JustFiction Edition

Imprint

Any brand names and product names mentioned in this book are subject to trademark, brand or patent protection and are trademarks or registered trademarks of their respective holders. The use of brand names, product names, common names, trade names, product descriptions etc. even without a particular marking in this work is in no way to be construed to mean that such names may be regarded as unrestricted in respect of trademark and brand protection legislation and could thus be used by anyone.

Cover image: www.ingimage.com

Publisher:
JustFiction! Edition
is a trademark of
Dodo Books Indian Ocean Ltd., member of the OmniScriptum S.R.L Publishing group
str. A.Russo 15, of. 61, Chisinau-2068, Republic of Moldova Europe
Printed at: see last page
ISBN: 978-620-3-57625-2

PHOENIX: METAMORPHOSIS

Table of content

I.   Phoenix

Nature is a master, a phoenix for regeneration

It stores, restores and springs up for rejuvenation

The flow of gold enrobing sunset is a sunflower

Turning slowly but surely towards the west tower

Looking violently toward the sun; for at least its backlight

The astral trail that lovers follow for radiance; is a taillight

That puts its poetic clams on feelings, an ultimate butterfly

With wonderful colors and a show off in a valley of firefly

Love polarizes every sermon; tributary to an existentiality

The spirit starts migrating toward flesh, a pure sensuality

Love is a resplendent, swarming temptation

A corridor towards feelings that set in motion

Lightheartedness, life soaring with smiles

All become a convention to wander miles

In search for the galaxy of bliss even in shadow

The elf told us to look rather inside the rainbow

To go far at the end of the avenue for the charming sunset

Picturesque, it is a joyous beat of jazz humming in ear set

"What a wonderful world" with Armstrong first in the heart

Each beat is a visual representation of colorful beads; no hurt

It is a merry soul that lets himself hit by the rhythm's prime

Smiles blossom, hammering cadence in the morning rime

Setting the pace for glee

Love enables one to flee

With wings to fly high reaching heaven

Through tune bits heard only in a haven

Of musical peace; a nonesuch location

Where love is a phoenix for regeneration

The human pacing nature is a phoenix for regeneration

When he is in love he fantasies, let loose his imagination

With a tremendous advantage over nature, he thinks

That alone sets the pace for being a phoenix with links

To do better what he has done before with a kiss

With subtleties to strengthen a wow without a fuss

Regeneration is a renewal of glamorous emotions

Reviving in the eye of a bed with new sensations

The environment is an aesthetic music to love

That is what is sung on tree tops by the dove

When love enters a soul, it chases away anguish

And any sadness that emotions rapidly relinquish

Nature incarnates the brut notion of pure harmony

The extra white snow is an infinite art through ebony

That comes after to see the seeds sown and blossom

Spring is the marvel of the revival of the phoenix's bosom

Summer appears with the call for nakedness and travel

The sun is its distinctive feature, showing to all its navel

Not willing to go to sleep even after nine post meridian

Up and bright, yearning to show off at six ante meridian

Every being stoops to its greatness and overt beauty

Leisure overthrows everything in this period of gaiety

All is spicy, the sage goes to rest under the sun's narcissism

A fearless and charming dream of eternity for this, his realism

That aims to stay forever but when with the equinox

The sun crosses the celestial equator; flora is no ox

It starts its silvery mutation sending humans shivering

For heavy comforters as the phoenix nature's quaking

In its effort to change the meteor's radiance and bring snowflake

The weather has its extremes cold and hot; this is really no fake

I usually turn where the horizon keeps secrets of all seasons

Everything, colors included change all time of year; as weapons

Of the magic of renewal showing the city, its outskirts

Under its various shades where the rise or the set flirts

With dyes, shades generating beautiful sceneries, mystifying

Like the owl unearthing an optimistic but gloomy ululating

Did he foretell death? Sure, but announcing a revival

Of the phoenix regenerating from it ashes for renewal

Helping fight ignorance wherever possible like a don

Ho! How I love the Canadian fall, the 'mascaret' in Moncton

Near Loblaws and the bridge toward a new life downtown

Music is a saver, with steps of dance my moral is never down

Stability is a drunkard's oath, the phoenix dwells in Montreal

Hills full of maple leaves and all colors on any tree top so real

Come some weeks later and all is 'gone with the wind'

Waiting the cold white snow for embrace and rewind

Purple, dotted green, red, crimson claiming 'love only me!'

Crushed with the weight of souvenir, 'this is the old me!'

Boasts nature that will afterwards strip all in a moody change

But autumn is not just a utopian cloth to charm for revenge?

The four seasons are phoenix in a rhythmic decorated crossfade

From high burning sun with flowered leaves to colors that fade

And then disappear to give way to an astounding whiteness

Mega tons of white even on roofs; an icy heaven and coldness

With autumn, the season of prestige, colors and the archangel

Governing multitude of shades, writing the ritual of the angel

Stultifying in a talking exchange warm with beauty and fame

Conveying the longing for a joyous life in an outdoor game

Whispering to man and woman in reveries

Dream for elves, imps, heroic memories

Through eyes, sights, glimpse towards a heavenly earth

A privilege to the soul, symbols of richness coming forth

In the sunrise the flow of gold seems a dancing jerk

It comes back during sunset with strange lights berserk

That present a hazy beauty flowered with autumn flags

Purple fades while begetting pinky spots and gold tags

8

These sceneries draw the highway of love, melting hearts

With the nebula blue cover, anyone is touched by love's darts

It works at aurora as well as at dusk

Arises with the ivory light of the tusk

Love flourishes with the fading away of light

It flowers again with the coming out of daylight

Rosy colors showing out with creamy dashes

Love is thus a phoenix, reborn from its ashes

Night fall comes tenderly setting affectionate memories

As twilight sets the tone for night love and its groceries

That are kisses, fierce embraces with thousands of sensations

Dawn with the promise of sun sets the vanilla sky with emotions

Amazing fondling caresses alleviate the nightscape

The nightingale adds up to the romance; no escape

From the love scattering breeze spreading the news here

"Can you feel the love tonight?" it whispers everywhere

Gold sand at the seaside is the dreamed outlet

To make the heart linger for love and just bet

That it will live long to grow strong and be dove-like

It capsizes all for love feelings all over and the like

1.1.   Phoenix Caterpillar

Butterfly was caterpillar in dream and duty

In the purple night far away from beauty

Fantasizing to fly high in the azure sky

To catch the Milky Way when it passes by

And dance with the stars at night when they lit

Showing where do dreams come from, show grit

Weaving towers in the rear of the paradise

Before daydream comes over to dramatize

Embellish all the nightmares and solarize

Life with rays of sun glimmering on a cheek hatch

With audacity, a spark the child wants to catch

The caterpillar is the beginner's mind, dragon, phoenix

A delicate dream, a radiant chlorophyll eater to nix

As the caterpillar disappears to let go of the butterfly

Wings are for liberty, daring to reach the empyrean sky

The caterpillar is a clock that start the metamorphosis

With greed, eating all green leaves to become beauty's Isis

The initial impression is subject to change for the brightest

Every day of this false worm is an enormous challenge, a test

Be lenient, be patient like a caterpillar to become butterfly

Good should be patronized in the human, a kind of wizardry

Change contains an awesome force, a real momentum

For a better future there is a need to target the maximum

Actualizing true potential, overcoming obstacles, a focus

Redefining values, outlining utility; the pinnacle of genius

The heart of the wild is the butterfly, an allegory of self-creation

The essence of life is dynamism, dying to one way of appellation

A metaphorical death, for a rebirth in another one, ever changing

Between perception and construction for vital space and being

A new self, a natural equilibrium, in a psychological struggle

Found in the might of transmutation, we need to always giggle

The temptation is so tantalizing to enter the cycle of remix

Of reviviscence to come out like beads; a colorful mix

Nature is the essence of transformation

From a debrided galloping for formation

There are astral phases from crescent to half moon

From darkness to the crystal impression, a light boon

With the round mother twinkling, the attractive moon

That'll cross the village at an elegant pace soon

For a hallucinating life and thinking of a firefly

The heart of progress is the nonesuch butterfly

Full of hope to come out as a marvel and great, fly

High in the fields sucking flowers, buds like a fry

Reality comes days after and caterpillar is over

Wings deploy; magnificent once in the itchy cover

They were folded in the spiral caterpillar

Who knows they'll be of beauty; a pillar

So marvelous in their parade that heads turn

The flame of hope burning towards a real upturn

Earlier eating leaves, growing plump is now over

The bulging caterpillar rummaging for leaf is over

The hassling worm is keen to change skin for new appearance

Ending nomadic excursion and taking it into a marvel entrance

In the world of the airy, colorful to beauties akin

Tearing fiercely off the rippling racking old skin

One drum-beating-rhythm morning the caterpillar

Just had its metamorphosis and became a star

The intermediary between necessity and beauty

Arduously grown wings stretched in splendor hearty

Starts its fine revealing dance in the early sunlight

That's life, with rhythm; lifecycle with might and delight

The hustler's mind is bright, flaming, glowing from hope

He urges himself to become what is best in the scope

Who will suspect the beautiful butterfly as a former caterpillar?

Life is constant metamorphosis into a brighter being and no liar

It's a courtesy, a honeymoon first from male and female butterfly

Then the female left eggs to green leaves departs in a swift fly

From egg to a wiggling furry bug greedy leaves' eater

The caterpillar shed skins to fit its growth, turning bigger

Spinning silk, it becomes pupa, a chrysalis

With a dash of pride, a pint of passion; hubris

Hanging itself from a branch, nurturing and later splits

An inside turmoil that comes out and any single thing fits

Who can do this miracle apart from the magical nature?

There is first a projection into a nonesuch adventure

A phantasm of success lived as a veritable beam

The butterfly is a rupture with reality; but a dream

He is more likely to succeed as he fixes no boundaries

As it's an innate capacity to come out of the prairies

From a worm-like feature to a blossoming butterfly

15

First creeping, dreaded for itches to the ability to fly

He is a dragon, multicolor and a phoenix

A marvelous being elevated high from nix

Hope, life and pride oozing from his pores out

Daylight boasts to be the truth as night games out

The creature with stitches and hair; eating leaves

From its night, constructed its diurnal parade eaves

Before the open space, there grandiose grasslands

Where the canorous wings fluff, breezing in bands

The night conceals a treacherous envy of delusion

The lying and the near dying state of sleep, the illusion

The end of the day is contained in the beginning of the night

Moon and sun, sun and moon playing the game of knight

A perpetual phoenix game as one dies the other comes out

In the same kingdom, the sky; it's a come in and a reign out

Who said that the butterfly is no phoenix?

From grassing and creeping, it can a fly fix

Graceful, ensembles scatter over the field

As colorful as flowers below them they yield

Guild of insects gather to suck, a reunion held

To gathering nectar with no need of a shield

A fascinating theater they deploy; more flamboyant

Than a rainbow alive in the empyrean; very buoyant

There is a rebirth of the old self into the new one

Obliterating one from the other's route alone

Fading away with the coming out of the fiancé

Too shy to meet each other for the karaoke

It's destruction at life's service in and out

It's with the sun that comes the action's pout

The sun covers the totality of the psyches

Moon and sun; symbol of life and death pulses

For us to take the defense of a dualism

This is only a stanza for more realism

For the hysteric faked danger of love's lost

One lost and the other found again at post

Life instinct lives in both forever

That's why they all people revere

They all possess the protector's helmet

But only at eclipse they tactlessly met

With satisfactory hallucination; a narcissism

Each eager to depart out of vanity; egotism

Their traumatic potentiality lies in their intensity

The full moon turns some humans mad in reality

The burning sun sends men running for shade

Because of flames of its rays sharp like blade

With day light doubt and fear seem to disappear

Victory over lethargy send subtle messages rear

In the deep forest as dew fades away

Workers on path with footsteps find a way

To hum a morning tune, a melody to joy

With birds churning a refrain to the boy

Whose song made the men marvel for a butt

Yearning to hunt for any heart in the hut

The day is lurking like a seagull

Brewing white wine in the skull

Dream is delicate; it has to be nurtured to come true

Strive hard to live up excellently to your dream

Don't make your whole life a mere tern stream

Dream the meteor shining and sparkling in the sky

And come out a butterfly resplendent and glitzy

With the potential to fly high in the firmament flashy

A rainbow parade with poke and dots; all glossy

And dance with the gods and devils with beatitude

Drawn by a powerful wind to reach infinitude

The temptation is too psychedelic

To follow myth and its dared relic

To resemble Icarus and borrow wings

And hop to the sky with a racket's swings

Tempting to fly high and reach the sun

Which will melt down the pirated wings

Binging downfall, getting a delusive binge

Down to earth the brother in a fatal lounge

Metamorphosis is an intra-psychic cycle of dynamism

Which kick-starts new series of life in dysphemism

With the power and might of dreams and imagination

It is a critical, arduous work for a real deconstruction

Self-success is inserted in a pluralistic reflection

The spiritual space is yearning for new incorporation

Time is a predator who overthrows all his victims

Those of childhood's malevolence to new maxims

It is a renewal in continuity before the exile, before the rebellion

Before the departure, the ultimate one even for the great lion

The one in us that roars and conquers the wild

Excellent to subdue anger and plough a new field

Don't let the dream turn into melancholy

For treacherous interrogation and folly

Resenting the anger, turmoil of the angelus

A promise of life churning the guts to focus

Tracing the magical circle, a singular experience

A commitment to life and its miracles over trance

Shared values and confidence with reverie as luxury

But no penalty for striving hard to be well and hurry

To become what the heart dears most; a total marvel

A prodigy crossing continents for nectar, fresh and novel

New paradigm harnessing originality with its paranoia

What is new is queer and frightening under the sequoia

The caterpillar and the butterfly are life dimensions

The allegory of a rediscovery of the self's operations

Ceaselessly renewed with a human plural vision

Crystalizing emotions, his striving emancipation

The complex relationship to metamorphosis

A necessary change after the tempo of osmosis

A contingent destiny with the search for happiness

Aiming to power the flower in the heart for cheeriness

Fly! Fly! Beautiful butterfly!

Fly! Fly! Beautiful butterfly!

How many stages did you cross?

How many lives did you live gross?

Before your flower state and blossoming!

Phoenix of another kind; though charming!

II.   The sun

The sun is a polysemic vector where as a king

He rules over the world, almighty over all thing

Its mildness conveys care for the wind blowing

The moon can be gazed at without blinking

But who can stand to stare at the sun?

Its radiance is such we become nun

Humble and it immediately our gaze lowered

It's the astral power that reigns, by all revered

Head and shoulder above, he's all magnificence

Zarathustra, the great man is Sun in brilliance

Sign of plenitude, he osculates our emotions

Giving dreams light to conquer with life passions

Pushing human mind to its perfection

Auxiliary of virtue, mother of invention

It's under the sun that humans strive and succeed

Marvels are shaped out, future secured to feed

Poverty is the soul's servitude, the sun whispers

Raising spirits, emboldens and work prospers

The sun is dynamic power to transcend weakness

Even for Nietzsche who proclaims man's wickedness

And no apology for him as 'God is dead!' hitherto

The great star is still an emphatic God to grip on to

He confers this inquisitiveness tremolo and vibrato

It conveys the flame of resilience to hold on to

A tiny glimpse to our lust, optimism is the motto

An aphorism, a frame of action no one to hide in grotto

2.1.   Fine sunrise

Fine sunrise over the dormant village

Splendid time to foresee day's heritage

The rise of the sun, a cool sky walker

That will afterward be fierce as stalker

Running after human's children as they toil

Earning a living sometimes; eager to foil

Rays too fierce, proud as fire with good wood

Sunrise is the promise of a new day for food

Morning mist lingers a bit over

As if a good way for a make over

With the gloomy dark night forest

Which just went with the stars to rest

Bringing up more nickel into the arena

A calm sunrise like steel, a cool persona

To stay in bed when healthy is a deadly sin

Everyone goes out to put in toil his own pin

For a day long free of dots in sky till sunset

Everyone is striving to till his plot and bet

Hoping a good harvest for a fierce dancing episode

Freedom of action, a social dynamic for a happy period

In the village with drums and balans never at odd

Some local beer boosts up and energies load

The night last breeze slowly blows to beep

Dawn stars are hurrying, jostled to go to sleep

Aurora is a lone wolf howling to swallow the moon

Because if it hides it would have to do so till noon

The nearly hiding moon is an artistic conception

Beautiful like a pending luxury jewelry in motion

Its round beads hurrying for cover over this dawn

A big globule milky and dreamy, eager to get drawn

The sleep becomes a pensive, restless early state

A between-two distracted awakening to contemplate

Stretching lightness like a flower blooming from bed

With the clear day, the fields are a genuine flower bed

Sunrise is a big orange over the horizon like a dot

Early morning breeze is a promise for a happy pot

Of stew ready with sunshine at its best, at peak

A happiness; faces with smiles all over that leak

Man is an imitation of nature waking up for his bread

While the cosmos stretches its hands toward the bead

The big round sun carroty is a real creation of heaven

That raises hell for humans who considered it a haven

Its zenith is the only problem; in-between is the morning

Most of the times cool even under tropics, soothing

And the evening when all the venom of rays is spouted

Romance starts blowing in the air, equable, unheated

All is thought first, comes second volition

After work all that is sought after is oblivion

Of the hardship, the trek of life in the field

Beauty is a powerful force, and humans yield

To the attractiveness of the day and come out

The day is slowly showing up, lazily blooming out

With a fine breeze gracefully courting the meadow

Sneaking in the veranda, advising a fly to morning dew

The fine sunrise is a sight direct from paradise

A fresh lily smiling to the world like a merchandise

Woken-up by the cock with its cock-doodle-doo

Flattering the sun to show out for a bit of tae kwon do

The day is showing up, too shy at first and then bold

A beautiful lotus with rays opening little by little to hold

With the human eager to wander under the red sphere

A disc that grows bigger and bigger till the atmosphere

And the sun says hello to everyone, anyone

Sunrise has wings to fly far away and alone

Mounting on its horse; the dazzling light speaks

The language of reheating the heart to its peaks

Cannot bear it no longer and grows shadows everywhere

Multiplying skirmishes, hide and seek with crepuscule here

A ferocious tiger it becomes at noon

Roaring and given to rays the toot tune

Influenced by the wizard of its company

Drying up flour and vegetables to accompany

The fire bewitched, the jungle seems entangled

In a mirage where dust is the mist; all strangled

The lion totem of the village hungry is roaring for a prey

Finding none it waits for the shepherd eager to secure hay

From thirst also, the star of the savanna is blinking

The real force and symbol of power is smirking

The king of beasts sounds like a volcano erupting

Everyone is on guard, the night can be very menacing

The curious owl opens big eyes and hides in deep bush

No soul to be seen wandering in the air for its smooth brush

Fine sunrise erases disillusion and insane desire

It's a dialog a temporal quest and decisive inquire

2.2. Sunset

Sunset starts like a lie

It colors the sky like dye

Progressively whitening the corners

Bringing broad daylight to turners

The evening breeze is refined luxury

For dreams of a fantasy night's drudgery

This a warm sunset, with sun rays lingering

A sunset like brushed by a painter flowering

His canvas, blossoming sprouts; on a side a mussel

A décor for the enigmatic night erasing the nickel

A blond platinum fading into metal and then black

And the changing moon will put her gown with slack

An orange show at west and the sun goes to rest

Dusk seems an old comrade to wait for the best

Blinking like an old bulb courting the night

Weary in a life giving process, a perpetual fight

It comes with a progressive hard graphite

Speared by shooting stars like stalactite

Colorful feathers become brilliant and golden

And appetite of love grows for emotions to raven

The crystal rises and wonders under the eiderdown

Never to fathom the absurd side of life and let us down

There is lust for the peacock's feathers and no dribs and drabs

For the virtuosity of seduction plain are the amounts he grabs

Tempting the partner; it is the right time for gallantry

Everyone knows that a love night is a sunset in courtesy

A starry sunset with melody, romance in the air

To feel love is natural and healthy, in life that is fair

Sunset makes the ocean yellowish and purple to the eyes

Flow of gold is a mystic trail to follow, catch before the pies

Free clouds accompany the sunset for free dreams

The night is the fantasy magnet attracting creams

The mattress is a planet with ripples like on the river

But it doesn't prevent from flying high and to rover

It keeps the flame of hope burning for love and supreme

Like an ancient rhyme, like glee galloping to the extreme

Towards an end that finally comes for everyone

It's lenient only for a moment, forgiving no one

With the dandelion blossoming while not far beneath

The angel is playing flute for someone underneath

The boastful human doesn't know that the end will come

Crystallizing desire and anguish for metempsychosis; a dome

Where the pride is in the soul and the spirit is a lion

But never forgets positively the action of the dandelion

He has the same might as the feline king that is cool

A redoubtable ability to subdue and supplant the fool

Sooner or later we cross the lagoon to let the bitter go

Replacing the need by desire, a longing for the alter-ego

With smooth riding or fiercely like possessed by dementia

Sunset is fipples and ripples over the river clad in regalia

To paint rapidly the fading day before it melts in black

As if the power in the orange won't again come back

Sunset in the west is a fantasy

Glory of variant in reddish easy

Reddish yellow, orange like flame vanishing

Original motive of punch; a podium waning

The sphere extends its shade over the horizon

A zest of citrus; subtle vitamin colors in legion

Slowly it is a metamorphosis, in relaxed motion

Extracting smiles and laughter like a caution

To avoid the possibility of a backward movement

As there is no move but a clock like one; no reverso

With the mild weather caressing lovingly the torso

Cool is the illusion that the day light will stay forever

No, its itinerary reached the vanishing point ever

The carrot-like color vanishes into an enormous rabbit

The owl is already beating the measure, a frightened bit

The sun goes thus to sleep while appears the satellite

Earth's natural one, the moon shy at first it starts to lite

And the laughing child just points to the moon

Telling his friends that it's cheese at its noon

It lights up and go through the window and festers

All dreams that become nightmares to tell elders

As 'the sun also rises' east always just after dawn, a genesis

A phoenix, a rebirth for many and sundry; a metempsychosis

2.3. Sunset with Muses

The challenge of life is in the fight for inspiration

That comes with the wind and the Muses' passion

Lit darkness exists in the rise of the moon light

It emphasizes the sublimation of the starlight

A strange vigil in the night kept awake

The artist with Polymnie for a weird wake

While she is chanting dirges for the departed

He is painting ghosts and rapscallions deported

The moon crescent is so beautiful; with a star as a dot

It appeals to the decimator of dreams that shouts a lot

In the tableau, his picture has to be erased as he is bad

One needs to plunge his memory to pass through as a lad

When there is no dream, there is no stream of creation

To never be able to dream is equated to a real damnation

Muses bring back dreams in tiptoe; put a finger on my eyes

A voyage to eerie land; I long for a real meal with French Fries

Moonlit night is playing hide and seek with the cloud

Is it for storage or just a lust of air in the wild and loud?

Like the rumbling of thunder telling the story of the sun

Which will reveal all her secret to humans in the long run

What to wait for and forget to die?

A bright star, a meteor with a bean's eye?

As the wind brings all the scents of flowers

On the airy planet, dreams placed on top towers

An extravagant vagrant shows up with sand

To activate a symbolist tendency of sleep in band

This nomadic wind is no friend; an enemy to counter

To shed off the emblem of the villain in any encounter

Muses come with their water and incite the chant

Music soars to fill the air with a mood to enchant

I want the power of muses to transform foes

Into ugly crows ravening cruelty without cues

Because Clio teaches all and life is a remake

Erato coming back with a new era to fake

The novation but it's rather a revival of the pure old

Caliope bangs it to perfection in her poetry that's gold

To the memory because the thread cutter Atropos

Is ever ready for us overcoming Moires and Cronos

Happiness is an everlasting state

A feeling sought after to paste

Everywhere cementing it in any single life, a bet

Muses have a word to say in that concern; a debt

To humanity and to Sisyphus lurking, kicking out hell

With ruse to make life longer, sweeter in a nutshell

Because anyhow we all know that the end will come for us

Shorter or longer any life will taste death like Sisyphus

It will be a fatal morning, evening, at dawn or at dusk

Every genesis is a start with en ending pending like tusk

III.   The brain

The brain is the boss, never be at loss!

As it is at control with a hallucinating gloss

True to the axiom ever; to forewarn is to forearm

To learn is all to nurture wisdom; to plow the farm

Science sprouts from the intelligence to make better

All that was done at random is arranged to luck fetter

With abilities that fill the midget human

In the search of progress for all human

A thinker has a place in society; he is adamant

He succeeds in placing life above all and radiant

Turning him into a giant mind

Culture is knowledge to mind

For great performance in liberty and no ban

Anybody has a say in the society with a grain

To fill up this essential skull

Even teach to fly as a seagull

Filling brain with wit, knowledge that will serve long

We have learned in a ludic way even all night long

The brain is a good friend we have to shut off from Alzheimer

And continue to feed it till the grave, saying word to it in-hammer

Through speech, love, friendship, tutoring; obeying to learn

Learning is a constraint that frees us by what we surely earn

To change positively and deeply society; speculating

Unlearn, relearn, recapturing life when it is escaping

Through ages and experience; tiredness and boredom

When the human being feels useless even there is freedom

Life is to avoid ignorance that is equated to live a martyrdom

The DNA has the experience of ancestors stored in its kingdom

All we have just to do is awaken it through hearing and reading

Through successful teaching strategies; theories of learning

To learn is simply astucious, improving many skills

To be able to express all; pain, pleasure in all the tills

To counter obsolescence and take part in life battles

For nobody to mystify us through lies and mini baffles

Cultural encounters make life perfect through new acquisition

Social change is likely to build up happiness through perfection

When it is well planned and carried, accepting the superficial

Going deep in the belief of goodness to seek any potential

Blending knowledge, seeking dreams to interrogate power

That knowledge bestows on us the device to build up the tower

Not that of Babel but the ones urging for concord, growth

Language, communication, ideas are communities' strength

Ideas change all, they make the difference

A utile combination of a consort occurrence

That brain in network translates into sundry advantages

The value of knowledge is obvious through life stages

43

Learning is a complex ritual that increases productivity

Causing the brain to multitask for a more honed ability

It's a creative field opening enigmas; an idyllic open space

With a unique creature; the human with his drifting pace

But also an eternal comedy of lost and found memory

Where trans-humanism wants the brain to win eternity

By harnessing technology to beat up death forever

And erase its recollection like a nightmare to be; never!

Intelligence algorithm is here to favor perfection not to fetter

The human uses artificial brain to make things ever better

Is pluralism an obstacle to human unity?

Is homogeneity a barrier to humanity?

Self-related learning can be the panacea

Life-long learning a necessity, a true idea

That carries out to wonderland; an empowerment

A challenge to a critical praxis in the environment

To learn is to challenge the status quo

It kills Hobbes and resurrects Rousseau

The key to general harmony; an echo to concord

Is brains together to create a dreamed real accord?

Hobbies cultivate humane ways of learning

Shared passion for painting and précis writing

Develop new skills in fishing, drawing

New ways of doing old things; exercising

In the open air, precursor of talents and new vocation

Hide treasures that confirm abilities started in vacation

Witnessing freely the gap between reality and dreams

And means to fill it by persistence and desire, no screams

Social games train the brain, the grey matter

Mentoring kids, adults and all not to ever falter

In the search of skills, reasons and ways to overcome

In all cognitive fields, striving to be precursor and become

A talent, with positive impact on life; boosting brain power

Resilience is crystallized perseverance for influence and flower

Know-how with humanist values, new pathways, fresh horizon

Everyone is a genius, for Einstein the intuitive mind is sacred zone

A gift while the rational one is a faithful, realistic servant

Society honors the servant and forgets the intuitive vagrant

The brain should use and praise both intuition and rationality

The world relies on cooperation; imagination for new reality

Any obstacle set in the way is countered by new brain deacons

Life is a prophecy for the beautiful, young and the old absconds

There is no speculative ethic as axiology is essential

Power is the ruler of the world; it's often so demonical

But fallacious rhetoric kills the strongest human

It confers ruse catapulting norms of a silly man

Socioeconomic intelligence fuels systemic equilibrium

To make life a delicious journey as joy is its premium

IV.   Intimate Emotions

Offer me love all wrapped in intimate emotions

That show through daily behavior velvet motions

Cues to where to go, what to bestow on the lover

A stream of sweet beautiful fantasies where to rover

As Disraeli put it, 'we are all born for love' and we cherish

This 'principle of existence and its only end' we all relish

The power of thoughts is mesmerizing

Feelings are converted into words enticing

The human, tempting him to be good

Backing up actions to turn into food

We are what we think but also what we eat

These become habits putting us up on feat

Intimate emotions are sometimes to chastise

To shut out bad thoughts, nightmare, treatise

For they turn you out much more into a villain

Dyeing dark a life with habits you erase in vain

That stay as character and become destiny

That is the reason why any deviance even tiny

Should be watched; systematically deleted when wicked

Changing stereotypes with critical thinking an evil evicted

Ontology is the transcendent incarnation of common good

Outcomes that satisfy everyone's interest in human hood

Our intimate emotions should privilege what is human above all

To love and cherish, be inclined to merry making be but no wall

Be rather a bridge, a junction of many roads

Collecting experience to build a passage to toads

Any life is sacred; it matters to humans and god

In charge of security, care for all, do well as a pod

Hold fast to your best conviction

Life is self-praise; a real dedication

To oneself, to the society and the cosmos

The art of being powerful wants no pathos

Harboring goodness and compassion

Here and there, throughout any fashion

Act according to thoughts you are committed to

Not as bad experience, scoundrels commend to

Foster ethical, empathetic thoughts everywhere

Be fair and sow seeds as you don't know where

The flower of goodness and abundance will blossom

Love is heartfelt but let it be seen taken on the bosom

Child, lover who are lamplight to our darkest mood

Truth and passion oozing out and with abundant food

Create an empowering mind to fight social dilemmas

The challenge of plurality is multifold even in pajamas

Restitute the sense of social values to all individuals

Satisfaction through generosity not in the use of vials

Be firm but good as you have to respond to yourself

By reducing prejudice and delve deep into the self

First and afterwards to family and the world

Bad habits die hard and leave stigmata in the fold

Of human life, dirtying it forever

Be good to anyone to profit better

From a life which is delight with people together

Comfort the positive in all yield a life; one healthier

Intimate emotions opine that life should be about love

Understanding, the crucifixion of cruelty for a dove

Colored with the 'milk of human kindness' exuding

Any ruffle or open war will be extinct in dialoguing

Collective marred identity concocts common fears

Laming norms that beget nightmares and spears

Down some emotions of complex societal rule

Culture inherits those worries under ferule

Good shared potions make strong communities

Around a soup or a marriage viable become entities

Primordial in mobilizing everyone, a paradoxical experience

Masks are worn to protect and bravery a hidden reference

Intimate emotions are the ideal melodies to nurture

Through tales and fails, audacious drives for the future

It helps with the rhythm of change and the swiftness

Of confidence within society for change effectiveness

Humanism is an art of living

A constant struggle and learning

To keep uprightness a common concern for life

Anywhere and anyhow, humanitarian fighting for life

Theirs and the locals while gunned down by intolerance

Dramas in Niger, Mali and Burkina show human deviance

From those intimate emotions which are taught since cradle

How to end up this absurdity and freely in the world paddle

Through cultural practices with solidarity discourse

Empathy and leniency should be offered in a course

The human is center and measure for everything

He should stay heart and head for soothing

This human duo hones feelings to screen out apocalypse

Erasing blind faith ahead, dire ideologies should eclipse

Intimate emotions should be therapeutic

Lukewarm, cold or hot but always empathic

They cure wounds; are music to the very heart

Empowering the weak to be valiant brave heart

They cry in clamor the dead with the neighbor

Galvanize joy with the lucky and soothe the poor

V.   Berlin Wall

A wall, an isthmus between two brothers

Has been elevated steadily while it bothers

All the souls in the country and beyond even

While the essence of the being is never even

It is in perpetual self-change and renewal

The static and unchanged is the new wall

While the world needs a freshness splash

And a lightweight atmosphere with no lash

In 1963, the dreaded serpentine wall, made its way

Separating like a devil the city of Berlin with sway

Bearing the stigmata of the cold war, a villain

The wall bears the grudge of carnage; it's certain!

A bloodbath known by all in this age of after war

Level of reflection and thought elevated forward

Too many dead men, but can a wall erase bitterness?

The heart must talk to another heart in kindness

The cold war embodied in a cold wall

Separating in fear a nation, brothers; all

Sisters giving each other a cold shoulder

With watch tower and guns and we shudder

No trespassing!

Soldiers harassing!

Must the fear be stronger to halt dialogue?

The wall of fright stands between as a rogue

This era is symptomatic of suspicion, caution, mistrust

Our memory is to erase a terrific war, but there is distrust

What the wall lacks is compassion, understanding

It was all about command and control pending

Empathy has been overlooked

Fear stretches to be overbooked

Dying to one way of warfare for rebirth with a cowhide

Instead of openness, a wall was designed to hide

Fears, a status quo deleterious between winners

An endless barricade of sadness, wrath's forerunners

Tatters, open wounds, bleeding hearts on each flank

No trust as people want to keep moving but no prank

The mood is actualizing an endless trauma, anxiety over all

Fragility cannot be combated with fear and a concrete wall

A lack of coordinated analysis shut space for debate

That of compassionate, caring philosophies to combat

Building watch towers to spy on the enemy, the brother

It is war the common enemy; it's over but to bother

Its disgraces are scar faces, walls the mastermind

This fence is an implicit bias to occupy the real mind

As the brother is as such no foe but a human

Who needs a peaceful little talk man to man

To end islands of hatred with pending bitterness

For open arms to cuddle love and dreams endless

To perfect the world for a future full of happiness

Through keys to dreams and songs of cheerfulness

The cosmos deserves nothing but the best

After warfare, tears, bitterness and conquest

Tolerance is minding for the building of a new dawn

Caring, promotion for life diversity should be grown

But what to do to stop the killing ideology?

A wall never mobilizes all but shows a philosophy

Joint discussion enriches life, like flowers by gardeners

But a wall shutting away danger to be with sure partners

Is an illusion to shut out the trauma of Barbarossa

Assuring protection, an angry spirit; no step of bossa

East and West are progressive position of the sun

It should not be a dividing line for the share of a bun

The wall as an allegory of division was to be destroyed

Thinkers with a blossoming of humanism were annoyed

Yearning for liberty for East, West, North and South

They raised up like a single man to fight and sooth

Mankind suffering from its own nightmares

Walls and guns, shouts, shoots becomes fares

For intolerance still lingering with an ill-fated anger

Can a wall erected overnight stand as a power ranger

Materializing the end of suffering with no sharing?

Que nenni! Destruct the wall to let life free flowing

As everyone coveting his fears and sorrow behind the wall

Is possible war rebirth and it was the coldest one; an upheaval

A cold war is being on guard, thinking pacifically, not showing it

But anticipating outrage, fire and how to promptly anticipate it

There is no peace of the heart, only caution and precaution

Dreading one's own shadow, hunting the devil of adverse nation

Trying to anticipate the first blow but no systematic violence

Still there is this clanic cyanic thought full of malevolence

Minding one own business and always ready to retaliate

The imaginary full of ambient imps, red threats the heart ate

You just like your brother, but you fear him at the same time

Tiptoeing and spying every time; peace time echoes war time

Conflictual transactions give way to dialogue and accord

The red telephone is a way to break silence on board

The cold war is no coward but it shuts off the brother

Colors of life comes with union, reunion and laughter

While minding about a future without war, no tear drop

For this there are vigils all over and spies to eave drop

Pacifists mobilize to reshape a new unified Germany

A dialogue had been instated to unlearn violence for many

By relearning to talk, to rebel, to raise consciousness

About the same red thick blood running with boldness

In any single vein of humans throughout the world

Heart to heart talks reheats coldness, with peace bold

This gave confidence to denounce the wall

Its cruelty within a single womb; those who fall

Are buried in this same earth that cries for peace

With bumps and fresh sand erected on its face

As a mother for all it doesn't want any bloody corpse

A fresh world is one of real harmony; never fierce

Freedom of choice should prevail for dwelling East or West

Erring freely for an intimate soul mate wherever life is best

Not constraint that humans hate in a metaphor of a wall

In a rage to shed off war flames and build peace for all

The dream of evasion hates wall; any barrier

Invasion is over, give way to the peace carrier!

The air is a perfect match, for the concept of freedom

A distinct form of exerting free will wherever, at random

The essence of subtlety, peace lies in real liberty

No mirage of reconciliation but quick certainty

To live and wander free, no alert survival instinct

The warmth of a heart should be in any precinct

To be free or not to be at all, is men's motto

Sowing peace you harvest greatest love hitherto

The wall is a nightmare, for protection, it's vain

Defacing the world, it is rubbish, many lives ruin

And many die for it while trespassing the fence for liberty

Because a wall symbolizes the end of the will to joviality

It says stop to dream and barricades the mind

That yearns for evanescence with a variety to bind

Space is among fascinating choices this is essential

A rain shower of elections, selections to live free is vital

A touch of singularity to shine more for adoption

Love blanket is a sunshine with rainbow's attraction

To fit the individual and wherever he wants to go

The desire to wander and wonder; always on the go

The perpetual evolution is fueled by life and freedom

With no temporal or spatial walled spirit as a kingdom

The world aims to be a smart box

A free spirit for a smart control fox

Let's go beyond the stereotyping mind

And never have gloomy thoughts but find

Always a motive of interchange, negotiation

To roll over the rock of war; install cooperation

Around an exultant meal to chat and chatter

To harbor no wall in heart to materialize after

In hard concrete, adventurer of melancholy

What the world needs is a new era for a folly

That of endless love and tolerance

Joke and merrymaking in prance

Building bridges and wiping out the wall

The world, the color of a European fall

With a fine sunrise over the world; East and West

Harmony is the empire of worth in which all invest

Break any wall to restore the freshness of the universe

Focusing on where empathy flourishes really in full verse

The hypnotic scent of liberty to wander

To permit to anyone to marvel and wonder

Everything is relative to culture, a subtle overtone of generosity

Are what's needed for the interpretation of the world is its reality

Its very powerful essence, seizing multiple qualities

Boosting cooperation for perfect harmony testimonies

VI.   Relaxed dream

The ideal world is led by people's relaxed dream

One is taken on a relaxed tour with all over cream

For those who like other rolls there is place to scream

Our choice whatever it is, in order to fly and over dream

With the constellation of stars in the sky as a single team

To the sound of drums like in a procession to the stream

Dance light footsteps made the relaxed dream perfect

Smooth is the pace of that starlit night with no defect

Hiding dark secrets in the heart of gleam; of nowhere

The city night air flirts with the envy of elsewhere

A relaxed dream got lost in self-compassion

To ease-up the tension of stressing perfection

Cutting oneself some slack in the sidereal space

The human as the real value with his free pace

Considering mistakes and any failure with gentleness

This means empathy, to be 'full of human kindness'

Erring is human, true; taking it easy is a kicker

For a harmonious development; socially richer

Negative stress regresses while optimism comes forward

With a wealthy life filling joy and flowers en any given ward

Relaxed dream is energizing when confronted to challenge

Work becomes leisure and is performed dreaming of lozenge

Deadlines come and fly away with heavy workload

In any color one wants his chameleon or toad

Everything boosting the ego is taken into consideration

You do what you can with a dose of self-compassion

To take care of your precious heart through a break

You are the essence; nobody wants you to be a freak

Tomorrow is another day to improve performance

All you need is love to be creative and full of romance

Otherwise, what if you have a nervous breakdown?

World goes on without you, shaping out a new dawn

When you are out and done for good

You become worthless with a fierce mood

Get less anxious about blunders and the terrible boss

Your health is more important than his head loss

Through worries and harsh criticism, swim out

Like a fish in his river slaloming in his hereabout

Relaxed dream is about feeling good, having fun

While striving to achieve goals, aiming like a gun

At your target, with a better mindset and focus

Think progress and relax like following a locust

Boost your motivation through small wins

Shed off your culpability and small sins

Don't raise your blood pressure for the unattainable

Forefathers were here and are gone unbeatable

'Life is a comedy', your role is to strive to do your best

Easing tension, dancing bossa-nova to avoid any pest

Stressors are to be relinquished in the rubbish bin

Keeping violence at bay, like a cruel dog is no sin

Maximize gains and minimize stress, avoid burn-out

Through relaxed dreams is a key quality, don't get out

Feeding fears and anticipating regret is pessimistic

It harnesses dark clouds to mar dreams; it's dramatic

Thinking big picture gives energy, a powerful fuel

It is a liniment to some episode of life that are cruel

The postmodern world is with technology extremely easy

But also harsh on the soul if you don't take it easy

Self-compassion is being a good mother for oneself

To make the world look like the best place to ego and self

To pamper the ego through small treats to keep happy

'Don't worry, be happy' is the best tune it's never floppy

Mollycoddle through hobbies to pump much oxygen to the brain

This is gaiety for the heart and it's full of joy and harbors its grain

Have the power to shed off negative thoughts and the boss

The soul should be a leisure city, accepting critics and the loss

That is temporary whatever it looks like

Every single day, the sun rises east alike

And build up a new era through perpetual change

Shift to more humane ways of working as a gage!

For more comfort in any work or role

Relaxed dreams urge to sing a carol

To find glee in a distich, rock and roll

You'll be elected in any soul through poll

Evade through a tiny idea like Alice in Wonderland

A longing for passion to cradle, wander in Graceland

Craving to make the most out of our compost

For a mindful and better like to parade and post

On social media for everyone to see and praise

Compliment makes life sweeter towards paradise

Self-compassion is to embrace with good impact

On life, a revolution on the soul; rewards in fact

With talents at stake, in life puts cream

One is to let go and be taken on a relaxed dream

To the balan's air beats, a convoy to the stream

Smooth is the pace of that starlit night

Comes along the healthy breeze with might

Hiding dark secrets in the heart of nowhere

There is a couple starting new life somewhere

The village moonlight's zephyr flirts with love

With the sky and the twinkling stars above

As witnesses of a pact, a love concordat to ease

And feed the starving affectionate boy and release

A lot more pheromones increasing the very magic

Stealthy shadows hum with the night breeze mystic

All is metamorphosis with the red charming purple

That was moments before a hiding green, supple

The heart growing wings like Icarus

Reviving to life and love like Lazarus

Love borrows feathers to take off

Flying away from tyranny dreaded off

And falling in the deep green forest

With its carpet to relax; a real full rest

Life is a souvenir that scratches sometime

The mind and the subconscious at bedtime

Like a pineapple with its green leaves around the neck

It's rather a light kiss some days after accepting a deck

With a forlorn touch like the devil's embrace; an hypnosis

The wizard of Oz sees here no dose for phagocytosis

Relaxed dream is never lethal, it's a recovering touch

Whatever the case, I'm a peacock parading to vouch

Paradise on earth with butter on bread

And marvelous multi-color feathers spread

Struggling to keep on track with demureness

A smart being raised to conquest wildness

I'm sometimes the cool memory of sad reminiscence

Turning into a blossoming sun glowing with magnificence

Free of any hunter in the past; he failed to enshrine me

I'm a mystery of life intoxicated with freedom, a free me!

Courting the sky high, the moon is blooming

While the city, charming and people singing

Life is a corridor where there is no unity; defy

Scattered are aims and passions to reunify

You build up your world with heart and soul, indeed

Striving as in Olympics, 'altius, citius, fortius!' the seed

Of courage up brings 'higher, faster, stronger'; performance

That matches our dreams by making the most of life's romance

Fantasy heated with turmoil topped by the envy to persevere

Resilience comes along with efforts, hard work that is severe

But embellished now and then with a dose of happiness

To celebrate the hero by all or auto-adulation; cheerfulness!

Come by haters in gown of devil in lace

Ready to spoil all with a single embrace

Judas in a jealous dress and making face

In lust for souls to highlight his pace

Scattered like a broken pearl necklace

Amid hostility, make the most to be the ace!

My nice work, a studious building of might

Thrown, turned down like a sand castle; bright

Too shiny for them, they lit it up as a firework

Falling in elegant sparkles, flame teeth as a fork

Prickling fate's selection box for stardom

With beautiful patterns, I can see freedom

With magic, everything is rebuilt as a kingdom

In the mist of star-craft and air waves; no martyrdom

Bravery governing my ears, enchanting my heart fully

Gold, diamond are nothing compared to my joy in unanimity

Recognized and praised a non-such elixir in all simplicity

Life is sweet 'a belle' like a Picasso in full ease in the city

It feels the air and gambles with the wind adamant

The night is turning into a cool dancing tournament

With silhouettes shaping out a black décor

There is nothing but acclaims to be grateful for

That's the rotating paradise's entrance with alleyway

Light in darkness is a forest to the heart to for anyway

Beat the rhythm of merry making like a monkey

This helps focus on the gorgeous lady; a honey

Perfect for a cuddle in a without brass mansion

All is gold and true to the little pebbles in fashion

The lady pampering herself with spot on cheeks and purple lips

Like she has received a quiet faint lip embrace, while in all; it slips

A boosted ego, that won't let me down

Recalling the dynamic glorious never frown

To shed off the single long and missed now fear

I never lack courage to work my way with no tear

Through life, through me as a shiny print

Carpe Diem, the rest of the making a sprint

In a life that wouldn't be true without me

I find way to leave my footprint a true me

Village remembrance sees fantasy everywhere

The lion even comes into my hut to rest somewhere

In my heart as the one called the lion-hearted

I'm the lion roaring, a mighty one; people flabbergasted

I can also summon enough courage to fly with the eagle

Exit the lion, comes along the elephant, a bestiary cycle

Dazzling as lightning, moving with magic and boldness

To set camp in my mind's doorway as a predator nest

I am and my mind is the mystic pyramid

With its lures and baits, a vacuum, hollow, humid

Partaking in a fierce war fueled by curiosity

Symbolizing the pharaoh ruler of a mighty city

Hell is bought, while paradise is free

Hell is bought with sins as you can see

VII. Fashion

The city is in constant fashion

Stars parading to be for a reason

Of a certain style; the point of attraction

Mode is a kind of life approach for seduction

In parade, strolling in beauty, fashion is passion

Under fireworks, light blue, purple celebration

Are on the stage for a radiant show

Everyone eager at the end for a bow

The butterfly radiance is about consecration

Any chrysalis to blossom as the model, a creation

The juke box is distilling an air, a music

Everything appearing glamorous, magnetic

In tune with the eerie deployment of wings

The fashion guru aims shooting stars in swings

Flowers catch the eye through the lightning

Dazzled with light, a girl's swagger is stunning

But it's for a parade's purpose, emotional turbulence

Is what the show is after through all this magnificence!

Life is a kaleidoscope, mirrors roaring with each ego

Every day's life in the universe is to be coped with and go

The spectacle, stands as a rotating meadow with green grass

Surrounded by splendor, many cloth style, silver, button brass

Gold glistering glittering through sweat in the night

There is a sense of perspective with in the air a fight

The beautiful is quite simple and the simple cool, not chubby

The texture of material, the poke and dot all concur and ruby

No bleakness, only a streaming reddish trail while pearls

With yellow strips and beach like sand are here Earls

Within a kingdom its decorum are bands of green and grey

The star is a dream, a one night stand reverie but also a prey

A cracker nocturnal is the night breeze blowing smoothly

Lost dreams are erring as a fault for new owners all in gaiety

To straighten them to reenter a reverie game with bravery

A big moon, emotional is forcing its way to enter the scenery

Escorted by star lights flaming like the sorceress' theater

Those styles are from the graphic art even tough brighter

With rectangles, triangles, quadrangles and no frost

A fickle geometry, one never knows where it shines most

Magic! By the way, what angle offers the brightest shine?

This flower collection is mimicking Mother Nature's shrine

It held the ideal of fall leaves in Canada; so beautiful

Any color brightly shining at its utmost, that's blissful

A luxury of brilliant sky line, strips of rainbow on earth

A kaleidoscopic sight bowing low to please the hearth

Who are those spectators clapping hands madly?

Stars and people of every walk of life certainly

Fashion is a meteor shining from the sky gleefully

Something that suggests length and forms eagerly

Revealing an art side sometimes unwearable

It enters the circuit of the imaginary and fable

The dearest side of invention wandering with elves

A revolution in form but idealistic with new sleeves

This other assortment is from the deep forest

Beauty is embodied by tall trees, colors the greenest

Flowers seen may be but the soil itself or a rare tapestry

Beneath foretells of a good harvest beside some pastry

Buds of plants are seen on the collar of the slender boy

For a kingdom in the sky the star parade is to all no annoy

There is a butterfly bunch on this fashion's bosom

One can sense the cool wind between trees' blossom

A lake stands where beasts are drinking water

Chanting the rhyme of freshness smoothing a feather

Life is a game to play or to catch

Really an on the stage show to watch

The mastermind of the show is the mighty

Elegant in a dark feather suit humming quietly

Pointing at a default on a model for a touch up

Style is a convention of the century lifting up

The spirit of the moment be it smart or foolish

But it has everything to do with frill to relinquish

The fashion boy has grown; he is now in old age

Cannot shed off his bright feathers an heritage

He became daddy cool, the dandy in him rebels

In an extraordinary dream of passion he still revels

Fantasy is luxury, lux is a state of mind dear!

He cannot let go of the magic of his best year

After the paradise lost it's the conquest of the stern grave

The spirit is yearning after the splendid times that rave

His sun is in heart and has known no evening plunge

Into darkness with shadows like robot, he is in lounge

Flirting with the night breeze forever with the stars

Fashion is a memory enshrined in time, nothing spars

From day dreaming till is blown the last trumpet

Showing of on Times Square like a squirrel, a pet

Fashion keeps a city roaring like a lion

Genial crown on a skeleton skull, an ion

Exquisite like a delayed mystery

That makes one shudder, no dreary

Luxury is a game of perfection in beauty

Of the soul but of art also nurturing jollity

It touches and transform the stern into a peacock

Or an envy of a gloomy gorgeousness, a bizarre lock

In the entrance of the imagination nonetheless flattered

A golden oxymoron to some and really wooed; courted

Fashion can be a monster, handcrafted with harshness

Towards the self to enter a corset that leaves breathless

This tyranny is to please, eating up all ease and defect

It's inventiveness for highly reinforced beauty effect

But who cares when you end up with a cancer, a sarcoma

For having pursued at your own expense a melanoma?

VIII. Halloween

Halloween! Allhallows Eve

Hello! All Saints' Day's Eve

Real children and those with a child heart lay

In wait of that long anticipated 31 October to play

November 2nd All Souls Days is to beg for 'soul cake'

With the freedom of choice in disguise, all is about fake

False queen, false demon, a wizard to fear; a skeleton

The witch is the most sought after design even in town

The celebration illuminated from different traditions

With Jack-o-lantern's folklore reviving in nations

The trickster and drunkard was up a tree top tricking

At last after a deal he succeeded in Satan's trapping

While heaven denied Jack entrance to its kingdom

As a heavy drinker and other evil deeds I fathom

In hollow pumpkins enter devils dancing for blight

Because of the cross carved on tree in fight

To reject the devil, Jack-O-Lantern rather a hero

Couldn't enter hell neither; as not totally a zero

The devil gave him in his realm the ember light

The lit hollowed-out pumpkin is a parody of this flight

From hell with the devil's gift, a single ember to find his way

Through darkness thus establishing the pumpkin carving sway

Halloween is about disembodied spirits wandering

To find an individual, a soul, to enter into this still-living

It celebrates the intermingle world alive and that haunting

Of the dead; so, a great feast, this connection reveling

Hide and seek with our fears and in us we tear the devil

It's an intimate conversation with revenants and evil

To better shed off the nightmares, everybody, daredevil

Celebration, Halloween feast is a peculiar custom, anvil

To hammer in the soul, passion for life by mocking rears

Parading in ghoulish costumes to purge own fears

Space and time are suspended to allow the dead and living

To converse and enter each other's world; but the still-living

Exorcise their fear of being possessed by spirit frightening

People go out to shout, stroll the city for trick-or-treating

Halloween helps us, a charm to our fears expel

Be the witch, the ghost and skeleton with a spell

But to trick for sweets we are frightened by telekinesis

The para-psychic is our try to shed out evil and a genesis

For a new being, out of the ghostly history and heritage

Lit pumpkin, sweets eating up all bitterness at this stage

Halloween! It occurs at fall, where the hour falls behind

While in spring it springs ahead but now cold is in find

Possible Indian summer going by, waiting for winter

But nothing frightens kids in king's costume or waiter

The season with the creative nature; autumn!

Colors flowering all over with fairy as the sum

Of this marvelous show off, opening Halloween

Forcing wide the imaginary for the soul to win

Halloween, a symbolic of a great human tradition

Audacious to face ravenous fears in a ritual function

Through reverie, fantasy enters an operating system

To decode what tears the heart with a fierce stem

A psychoanalytic perspective for free wandering of gist

To fraternize with the witch in us without coming to fist

Life is a battle of the mind to sort out our demons

Wizards, geniuses all coming blazing on summons

The witch is the predator to fear

A night, only one night in the year

Everyone is allowed to parade and pour out

What titillates his brain and makes him freak out

To release the malevolent magic and let go of his spleen

It's a positive outlook towards fears through Halloween

With the liberty to disguise into our spectra

On the continuum one can even be Electra

The world of images and supermarket intervenes

To open wide the possibilities full of rampant veins

Where crawl the crabs, the rats and nuggets

To set a theater for a full of numerous gadgets

From skeletons to weird green matter oozing skull

Cob webs with spiders creeping are the tale to lull

And enter the realm of the phantom, the walking dead

Green, grey from death's tortures without any mead

An analytic principle enlarging even the scope of witches

To include the step mother and mother-in-law with stitches

For every individual, it depends which spectrum can clutch

Flirting with a devil for which any human has on a crutch

Our fright lays in the very archive of the tiny brain

Before what Halloween dreads shall we refrain?

By the dynamic principle of mesmerizing our fears

Going smart giggling throughout streets without tears

We can rely on our deep terror to mend our weakness

Halloween is a blessing but awakens up wickedness

The nagging swagger is never far when the sorceress comes

A broom with a verruca on the nose; dark, the night becomes

Upsetting the norms of fear, adding grey to fill our inner space

The witch is a great healer, a great artist with a gloomy face

Pursued with the sneers of society, cached up with misogyny

The authentic authority emerges our might making fear tiny

The wizard has more malice and harm

He is hidden in man's power with his ham

Curiosity and intuition make the witch

The cosmological hurt of the very bitch

IX.   Words of meaning to us

Let's go out and paint the town red!

The Jula will say in this spirit instead

Let's go out and heat the town pa! pa! pa!

With steps of joy at the balan bala bala!

Using a drive-in mind like a steel trap

He grasps the language and gets to rap

To the drum beats and takes a step or two

He took to it like a duck to water, bowed too

After a night chant and dance

He looks like a million; for a stance

Approaching the girl's heart as a lion

Life is dancing forever till the dandelion

That every being would eat from root

The jealous, the tearful, the brave on foot

Will get down in the heart of earth dreaming

With the last music of life he's still humming

Anyone, smelling like a lily or rose is longing

To stay forever on this earth and keep drumming

But ever-ready for a lust voyage in a twinkling of both eyes

Wistful or rebellious the end is the ground; no French fries

It works like a charm for all; it comes soon

It happens to anyone once in a blue moon

But even if you don't have a red cent at all

You can take part in the street dance at fall

You have to go and greet ancestors by the way

That is what is obvious from birth on anyway

Death has something up his sleeve always

Even if you are cute like a button, it never sways

It will have its ways jerking or laughing your bays

Are there, your natural anchorage, paths are days

To cross for someone or his neighbor a farewell

To arms and to everybody even not ready, it's well

As death is a traitor, a real turncoat

Which comes and ends up the morning oat

He knocks any being out

And it's forever black out

Green is the peasant preferred color

The earth hatches this greenness; no pallor

Only the yellow, purple and rose flowers

Impose on the chlorophyll reign its powers

The human plays the role, this superhero

Who takes time to never calculate zero

Who harnesses the blue of the sky

Marvels, dance and all things magnify

That transforms and defies the key

To transcend and overpass the decay

The special light, clear blue of cloud

Stands as a song that speaks loud

Which when dark blue falls in water, flood

Washes all waste towards the sea and blood

Thicker than water flashes beneath fearless

Telling a lineage's story through a tree leafless?

All this water falling and trickling in earth

Catches the sower's wisdom's eye to unearth

Hone his genius for leaves to blossom

For the couple to placate on his bosom

The baby, proof of the good harvest

For full stomach, full happiness they invest

Mixing blue, pink, dark, life to make hope

Colorful, golden blinking in the sun of the Pope

Diversity is captivating, trendy and contains the world

A panoramic colored mirror for regeneration to unfold

Master of magic that sees the marvelous

All act in synergy to end the circle, vicious

That of the destroyer never fed up of soul

A love never ending that's true since Saul

X.   What it means to be human

What it means to be human

Lays in the folds of any man

It conquers with compassion the heart of any woman

As Erasmus sets religion aside to better serve the human

Through myths and allegories, renaissance taught kids leniency

Tolerance should govern the world or violence will end humanity

What mankind with humanism needs most

Is a commodity at hand no need to defrost

A tender heart which hatred and cruelty forever ban

Is the one to gain right away the adherence of life fan

Those who live are those who fight

Hugo told us this maxim that's right

Education makes the future bright

Acquiring knowledge is a real might

To be able to transcend joyfully, obstacles, set limits

Following progress and appreciating what it permits

Go further to be a better human who everywhere fits

Go beyond bounds, to strive; never be among misfits

In a world where kind-heartedness should be first

Struggling to fill the blanks for a real colored burst

Fighting for power can be good but stretched to an extend

It shattered up the basis of cohesion where we all tend

Life should be a creative medium with always a new design

Ferretting tradition and computer era for a true headway sign

To fit the needs of people towards happiness

A constant search for true comfort; stress less

In an original, universal or ethnic way according to desire

Dreams are the greatest designers of time; they truly inspire

The wish to renew the world according to better human trends

The social comes to the aid of technology and ignorance fends

A pencil and a sheet of paper to conquer the world

A proactive way for choice to engage in the wild

To change it for the best; boosting thus productivity

Life is about building bridges towards fraternity

What is human looks sometimes like marshmallow

A joyous, ludic outlook is a refuge against sorrow

The search for happiness is what it means to be human

It sings the poetry lines of gaiety and abundance in man

But life is a mysterious being nourished in good omen

An irresistible tendency for rustic chic with even a sen

Adding up to the archives of the brain

Sowing wisdom, knowledge, its grain

Souvenirs, paints and chef d'oeuvre guide to day with light

Issued through strenuous years of toil to perfection and tight

With morale for great orientations and priorities towards space

Fiat lux and this light should shine through for a cozy life and face

The adaptation of world's mosaic to the art of the soul

Must be established as a tradition not to be with the foul

Lord Baden Powell turns us towards the book of nature

For useful open air pedagogy; all its resources nurture

Even before the hieroglyphs on the soul is written

The upmost value of the human, above all that glisten

It requires equilibrium and interconnection

Intelligence for enjoyment, peace and excursion

Through the heart that should cease to be a desert

Rather a freedom choice to be for others a dessert

A prestigious past dies when its offspring neglect effort

The world is constant rethink to persevere in the fort

The fortification that secures everything for evolution

History, heritage illuminate life for an adding-up decoration

That can be useful; to be human is to embellish

Everything and have the soul embroidered childish

To fly high with dreams, imagination and the rain

A promise of pleasure with smartness nobody slain

Flexibility and total liberty to learn engenders no villain

In the mind's eye, humanism is all caring in the brain

What it means to be human is hedonism

Inspired by the search for pleasure; a heroism

Gives to imagination an artistic and prized dimension

Strive to heal the world, feed the hungry of the nation

Appease the angry, clothe the nude and cold

From icy nights and emotionless fights in the fold

Despair should be no more with busy helping hands

To turn anyone into a happy person with the bands

Humans are singular lives in quest of absolute

Which is none the less soluble; and socials dilute

A striving life coloring everything with dynamic evolutions

An endless adventure made of mutations, transformations

In this life, be happy for something and nothing

It's to be human to unlearn and relearn a thing

A profound link towards a help and good expressivity

Going deep in the creation to come out with sensitivity

Life, a social construction is really an on-going pedagogy

It keeps on constructing the human through andragogy

Consciousness makes people human not absolution

But rather a heart of care through active reflection

Accounted for good or bad, hedonism carry lust of happiness

Even war skills are transformed into peace strivings; no less

Different classes and abilities build a united society

It means that ideology is everything in the diversity

So sorting out the best one for societal living

Is the best thing to do to still enjoy everything

And that is what it means to be human; live better

Healthy, happy as ever; a village or urban dweller

XI. Child

A poem I've written some twenty-five years ago

The only hope he confesses

Is to be alive

The only dream he harbors

Is to be kept away from labor

Don't let the child's fate sink

But have an echo deep in our hearts

Let us fly high in our dream

To have a safe place for a child to grow

To provide him with love, the utmost need

For him to hum a song of affection not in affliction

Provide him with a school to struggle to learn

Not to survive

Little girl, little boy

Left alone in distress with the dirtiest chores

Where fate makes them land

They are not entitled to school

While they care for their mates

Born to the masters they serve

In the house of the rulers

They will never be class mates

Because their fate is to toil

In order to avoid starvation

For them are leftovers

For the kids of the house all the honors

Mistreated at an early age

Future for them harbors a dark presage

If ever the mistress didn't beat life out of them

Who cares about them, anyway?

Children' rights is a paper

The police is a crapper

Who cares for the little ones?

Placed in by the mother, the father

Tears in eyes

Knowing very well how the masters are

But the crops have dried

The sheep, the goat have died

Nobody must be left to consider the alternative

To put one's child, in the hands of a slave master

Only to see him be alive

The broker has taken the last cow

The shop owner has taken the last bicycle

That's dire life, its cycle

So they were obliged to go and see children' blood suckers

They'll knock sense out of them

Mistreatment pending but something to eat

Not to starve

Nevertheless, they were taken to them

Be good my daughter, my son!

Be good to the master!

Be good to the mistress!

The father left

The mother left

They cried all the tears of their body

While the child threatened cannot even cry

They show him the broom

But before the whip was shown first

At last the father's tears dried up

The mother's tears dried up also

Just like the crops

Just like the sheep

Just like the goat

Just like their children' future

Who wants to know?

Who cares anyhow?

From the mother's bosom, the milk has dried up

No cow anymore to provide some

The baby altogether has dried up

The smallest child he followed has dried up

His skin has crackled like that of the earth

His eyes has sunken like that of the cattle

They dug a shallow grave

To put both in

To confide both children to the earth

With their crackled body don't they look alike?

XII.   Steve Jobs, a hero

His motto was: treat yourself well

And others alike before farewell

Apple the symbol, to the world a revolution

A perseverance, the iPhone an icon, a revelation

Mobility brings about ubiquity, a breakthrough

Internet is the world at one's doorstep though

Life is an enchanted instant to be filled with research work

A productive tension for reward in magic for firework

All in one, phone, camera, the web; mystic icons

Steve shaped out pinnacle of achievement for tycoons

Multitasking, coping with numerous things simultaneously

Love never loosing track of us, for we are here spontaneously

Friends and foes are real happiness

We shall educate children to find gladness

In every stride to court knowledge and ignorance sue

Through hard work knowing of things the value

Pricing a life of resilience, the essence of success

Failing once is an ambition for quest, ultimate, endless

The blue box, iMac, iPod always paying court to perfection

Even rejection creates determination, no crippling emotion

Being human in all action, wooing with elegance the sunlight

The hypocritical and base human cannot cease the fight

In a striving heart, the son of Adam and Eve

With the bitten apple has conquered, at the eve

Of a technological era, a kingdom; he's simply the best

With a global device, shaped for progress in a single nest

Symbolic logic includes those social intimate chronicles

They trigger the fantastic and find what is hidden in knuckles

Trapped in dogma, never! Be a hustler in what improves health

Is the best thing to do, as money can sneak in and out; wealth!

Apple, a logo to go a long way through the cosmos

Eureka! Smart Newton under the apple tree is boss

Inspiring Scientifics and humanists for excellence

Apple 'Let it be'! Produced the Beatles in magnificence

Add knowledge upon others', to build a better world

Steve Jobs is here to stay in mankind's magic fold

Ultimate world changer, the computer is creativity

Doing wonders from real innovation, originality

A courageous heart to share one's dreams, a fight

Details matter in a great job, endless search for light

A keen eye for perfection; Jobs, a bold innovator

The bitten apple forever, the legacy of a bold creator

With a pancreatic cancer he went away to stay

With the stars in the firmament, surfing the Milky Way!

Printed by Books on Demand GmbH, Norderstedt / Germany